SAUDI ARABIA

SAUDI ARABIA

MARTIN MULLOY

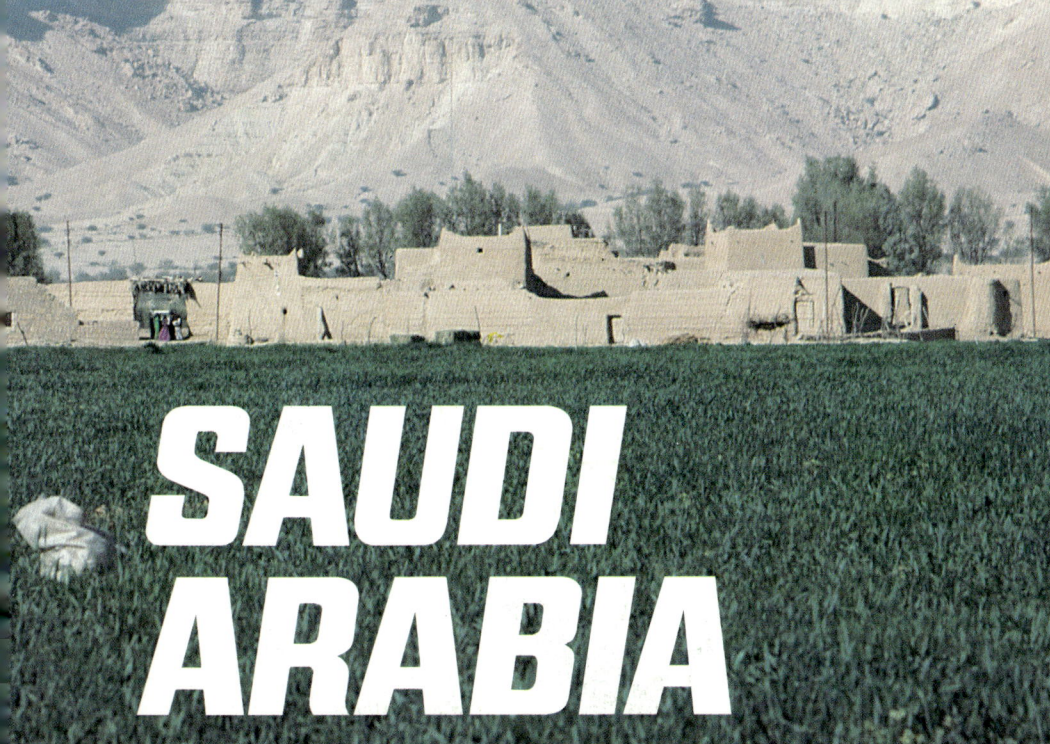

ACKNOWLEDGEMENTS

The Author and Publishers are grateful to the following organizations and individuals for permission to reproduce copyright illustrations in this book:

The British Library; J. Allan Cash Photolibrary; J. B. Free/Vidocq Photo Library; Hutchison Photo Library; NAAS; Popperfoto Ltd; Helene Rogers; Al Salazar; Frank Spooner Pictures; Travel Photo International.

Copyright © 1987 by Martin Mulloy

Published by Chelsea House Publishers

All rights reserved

Printed and bound in Hong Kong

First printing

ISBN 1-55546-179-4

Chelsea House Publishers

Harold Steinberg, Chairman & Publisher
Susan Lusk, Vice President
A Division of Chelsea House Educational Communications, Inc.

133 Christopher Street, New York, NY 10014

345 Whitney Avenue, New Haven, CT 05510

5014 West Chester Pike, Edgemont, PA 19028

Contents

	page
Map	6
Saudi Arabia: An Introduction	7
The Land	11
Islam: The Basis of Saudi Arabian Life	22
The Historical Background	31
Modern Saudi Arabia	38
The Bedouin	48
The People Today: Daily Life in Saudi Arabia	56
The Economy: Industry and Agriculture	68
The Cities and Towns	77
Saudi Arabia: The Present and the Future	89
Index	93

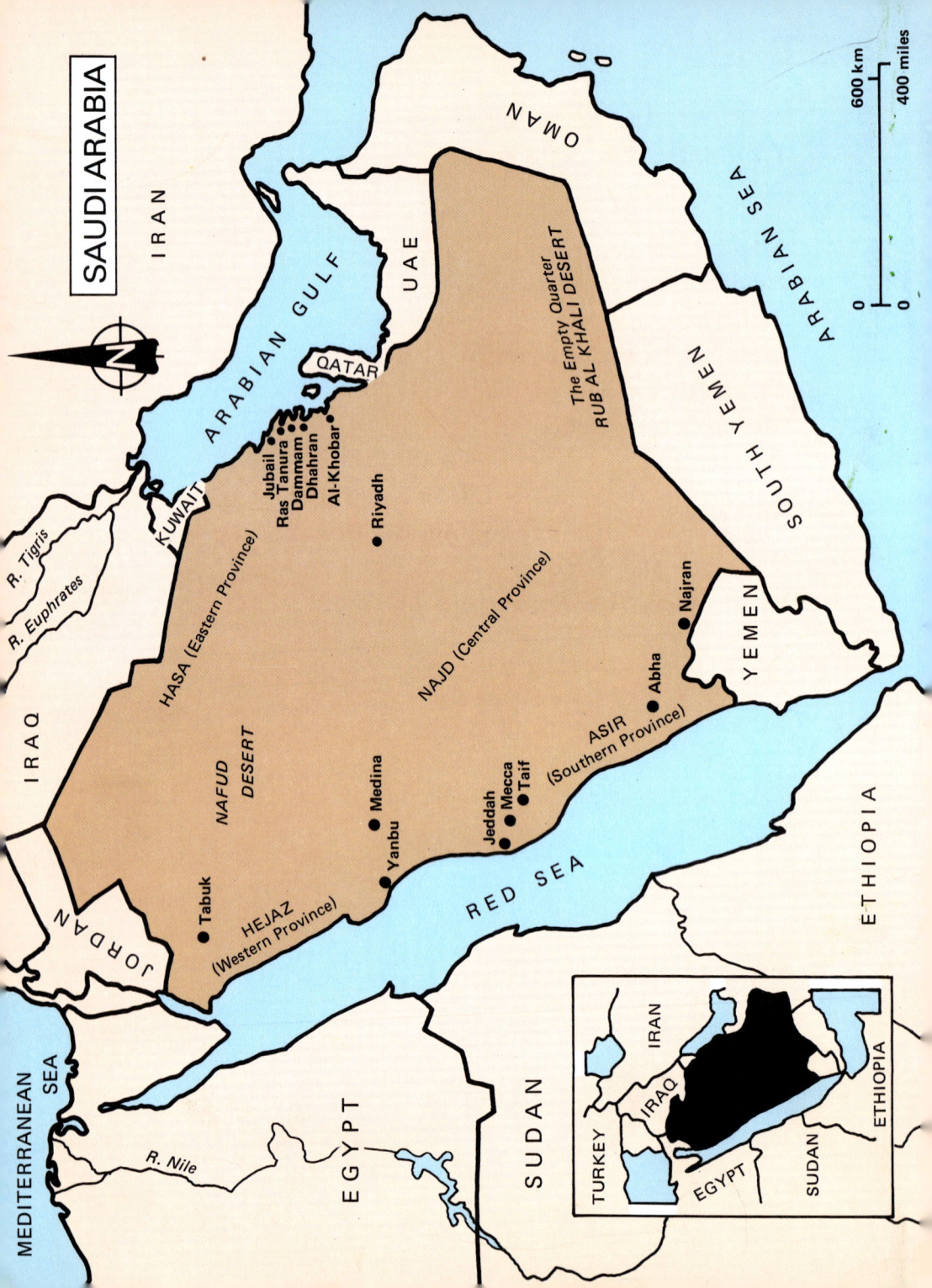

SAUDI ARABIA

Saudi Arabia: An Introduction

At the beginning of this century Saudi Arabia did not exist. Geographers, explorers, seafarers and traders knew of a landmass which they called Arabia and which they believed to be a vast and forbidding desert almost the size of a continent. Most of it was an unknown world: a secret land, the subject of travellers' tales. Some things were known. The ancient holy cities of Mecca and Medina had been visited by several Europeans disguised as Muslim pilgrims. The coastal areas and ports had been charted. The British Government had established protectorates in some of the ports of the Arabian peninsula. Ships which used the Suez Canal on their way to India and the East sailed down the Red Sea in sight of the hot and mysterious coastline of Arabia. Merchants knew of other ports and inland towns and cities where their cargoes were eventually destined. But still, even at the beginning of the twentieth century, the coastline and the ports were merely the fringe of something which was huge and unknown.

One other important fact was known. Islam, the religion which had swept most of the known world in the seventh century A.D., from Spain to central Asia, had its origins in this barren landscape. In the late nineteenth and early twentieth centuries, the Islamic Ottoman Empire of the Turks was still a major political force. The Egyptian capital, Cairo, one of the centres of the Ottoman Empire, was much visited by Europeans, hungry for exotic landscapes and antiquity. But, despite this, little or nothing was known about the land on the other shores of the Red Sea. Several adventurous explorers, from the Britain of Queen Victoria and the industrial revolution, had even ventured deep into the desert and returned with maps and detailed accounts of this mysterious world: a world of wandering tribes, the Bedouin, of desert raids on caravans of camels, of mud-walled towns and oases. For many people at the turn of the century, the name Arabia simply meant the exotic and the unknown.

Now, less than one hundred years later, Saudi Arabia is one of the world's richest and most powerful countries. It owes its name and its existence as a unified nation to the determination and vision of one man—Abdul Aziz Ibn Saud. His conquests and his rise to power began only as recently as 1902. His goal was to unify the distant and warlike tribes and to create a state based upon a return to a pure Islamic religion. Saudi Arabia's present-day position as one of the economic superpowers of the world is due to the fact that below the barren sands lies the biggest oilfield in the world. The first oil gushed to the surface

The ancient mud-walled town of Diraya, surrounded by date palms

in 1938. Since then the story of Saudi Arabia has been one of constant and dynamic change, as if several centuries of development had been telescoped into fifty years. Among other things, it is the contrast between centuries of unchanging desert life and the sudden headlong rush into the modern world which makes Saudi Arabia so fascinating.

Today the unknown and mysterious Arabia of 1900 is a country of strong Islamic character and of unparalleled wealth;

Saudi Arabia today—the old and the new side by side

a country which changes and progresses constantly; host to an international workforce from the four corners of the earth; and, finally, a country where ancient and modern exist side by side.

10

The Land

Saudi Arabia is a vast country. It forms the bulk of the Arabian peninsula, a huge landmass between Africa and Asia. The Red Sea lies to its west, the Arabian Gulf to the east and the Indian Ocean to the south. Saudi Arabia is almost half the size of India yet it is home to a population of only about ten million people, while India has a population approaching one thousand million. There are many reasons why such a vast land contains such a small population: the main reason is to do with the nature of the land itself.

In ancient times, this part of the world was known to the Romans as *Arabia Deserta*. It was considered arid, dangerous and of little value. The climate was a mixture of intense heat, hot winds and sandstorms. Travel within the land was impossible because of the burning temperatures, the lack of water and the hostility of the tribes who lived there. Little or nothing grew in the barren landscape and to outsiders, like the Romans, even basic survival seemed impossible in such a harsh and menacing

Contrary to most people's expectations, Saudi Arabia is not all dry. In some areas, like the south-west, there are streams and rivers such as this, produced by seasonal rainfall in nearby hills

land. Even today, Saudi Arabia conjures up images of endless sand dunes, hot cloudless skies, mirages and heat hazes—an environment fit only for scorpions, snakes and nomads; but this is neither a complete nor an accurate picture. In some parts of Saudi Arabia, travellers could be excused for thinking they were in Europe, perhaps in Switzerland, because of the Alpine peaks, cool mountain air, forests, streams and waterfalls. Only a second glance at the presence of date palms, orange groves, and baboons running over the rocks, would destroy the illusion. It is important to realize, therefore, that the sheer physical scale of Saudi Arabia permits a wide diversity of climate and landscape.

The area of Saudi Arabia is about 1.6 million square kilometres (1 million square miles) and divides into six major regions. These regions encompass dry coastal plains, wet and humid mountain areas, windswept uplands and, of course, vast tracts of desert.

Running from Jordan in the north, all the way down the Red Sea coast to Jeddah and Mecca, Islam's holiest city, is the region known as the Hejaz. In Arabic *Hejaz* means "barrier". Indeed, the distinctive feature of the Hejaz is a long mountain chain or spine which runs the entire length of the western region, separating the inland deserts and plateaux from a narrow coastal plain. Some of the mountains in the Hejaz, especially in the

The Hejaz, the mountain chain which separates the inland deserts and plateaux from a narrow coastal plain

A cone shell which fires a poisonous dart at its prey—one of the dangerous species which inhabit the coral reefs of the Red Sea

southern part near Mecca, reach heights of 3,000 metres (9,000 feet). While the area is generally very dry, thunderstorms can cause mountain torrents and flash floods. The mountain chain has many ravines and gorges, cut by these sudden and fierce floods. For most of the year these stony riverbeds, known as *wadis,* are dry. To the east of the Hejaz mountains are high desert plains and oases.

On the Red Sea side of the mountains, most of the land is arid and difficult to cultivate. The Red Sea itself possesses one of the world's most beautiful coral reefs. But in the past this wonderful natural feature has created problems for shipping, so that ports have been established where there are natural breaks in the coral barrier. The dramatic undersea beauty of the coral is not without danger; the reef plays host to sharks and other dangerous species such as stonefish. As its name suggests, the stonefish has the appearance of a piece of stone or rough coral; it has sharp spines, however, which are extremely poisonous.

Despite being hemmed in by a marine barrier and a mountain barrier, from ancient times the Hejaz has had settled communities in stark contrast to the nomadic peoples in other parts of Arabia. The reasons for this are varied. The coast provided people with an opportunity to establish fishing villages and to trade with Egypt, Sudan and Ethiopia on the other side of the Red Sea. Piracy also flourished in response to the seagoing trade. The Hejaz was also part of the fabled spice route from India and the Yemen. Travelling convoys of camels, known as caravans, would use the Hejaz coastal route to transport their cargoes of spices and frankincense. With the advent of Islam, pilgrims came regularly to the holy cities of Mecca and Medina, and trade and business flourished. Also, many small oases were to be found along the coastal route and these enabled small communities to settle; camels, sheep and goats were raised and a variety of fruits were grown. The oases owed their existence to the presence of underground water in the form of springs or wells. Even today, a significant part of the Saudi population

A terraced hillside

is concentrated in the Hejaz in cities such as Jeddah, Mecca, Medina, Taif, Yanbu and Tabuk.

To the south of the Hejaz, in the south-western corner of Saudi Arabia, is the Asir region. This is a mountainous zone which enjoys rainfall and sometimes even monsoon weather, with tropical downpours brought by the winds of the Indian Ocean. This area is often called "the garden of Saudi Arabia" because it is so green and fertile. The landscape is dramatic, with high, sharp peaks, juniper woods and green terraces lining the mountainsides. The Asir is rich in agriculture; beans, potatoes, tomatoes, wheat, maize and barley are all grown here. Tropical fruits such as bananas, oranges, grapes, melons, limes, figs and dates grow freely.

In particular, the date and date palm tree have played an important part in the life of this region, and elsewhere in Saudi Arabia. As well as providing food, the tree provides good wood for construction and the palms themselves can be used to make ropes, mats and baskets. It is not surprising, therefore, that in a land which is largely desert, the palm tree has become part of the national symbol: it symbolizes prosperity and can be found on present-day flags, coins, banknotes and coats of arms. To this day, dates are an essential part of Saudi Arabian life. After oil, they form one of the country's major exports.

In recognition of the beauty of the Asir region, Saudi Arabia has established its first National Park here, both to conserve

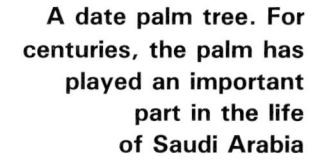

A date palm tree. For centuries, the palm has played an important part in the life of Saudi Arabia

the natural scenery and as a haven for wildlife. For many migrating birds, on their way from the cold of Europe to the warmth of Africa, it is a staging post on their long journey. Local species include eagles, vultures, hawks, owls, heron, ibis and game birds. Many of these are now protected. Other wildlife inhabitants of the region include baboons, wolves, foxes, jackals and hyenas, mongooses, leopards and gazelles.

Like the Hejaz, the Asir region has been home to settled communities, since the moderate climate and fertile land have allowed for the existence of farming and village life throughout history. In very sharp contrast, a short distance to the east, beyond the mountain peaks, lies one of the hottest and most forbidding deserts in the world—the Rub-al-Khali, or Empty Quarter.

The Empty Quarter is much larger than the whole of Britain and yet no one lives there. There are no roads, no villages, and hardly any oases. It is a vast sea of sand which constantly changes shape as wind and sandstorms alter the massive dunes. Like giant ocean waves, some of these dunes are over 150 metres (450 – 500 feet) high. It is practically impossible to live in the Empty Quarter and even to travel across it is a dangerous venture. It was only in this century, as recently as 1930, that a British explorer became the first European to cross it. Hardened desert Bedouin fear the ferocious heat and awesome size of the Empty Quarter. Even now any expedition in the area requires experienced local guides, water supplies, radio and medical equipment, special jeeps and camels.

Rolling sand dunes—the sort of landscape which many people most commonly associate with Saudi Arabia

This enormous desert in the south is almost mirrored in the north by the great Nafud desert which stretches from near the border with Iraq to central Saudi Arabia. One unusual feature of the Nafud is that, unlike the Empty Quarter, it experiences occasional light rainshowers which result in the sudden, overnight flowering of desert grass, flowers and other plants. In winter, both deserts can be extremely cold at night and frost is not uncommon. Summer daytime temperatures, however, can reach other extremes and 50 degrees Celsius (130 degrees Fahrenheit) is typical. In addition to the harsh, furnace-like climate, the desert abounds with snakes, lizards and scorpions. Many of the snakes, such as vipers and cobras, are highly poisonous. It is no accident that most of the desert has never been inhabited. The very landscape itself changes with the hot winds, and vegetation is so scarce that even the camel, the hardiest of desert animals, finds it impossible to survive for long. Inevitably, throughout history, the only population found in these hot regions has been the wandering Bedouin with their flocks, constantly searching for tiny pockets of grass, pasture and water wells in their effort to survive.

Between the great deserts of the Nafud and the Empty Quarter lies the area known as the Najd, the heartland of Saudi Arabia. Most of it is rocky upland with dry riverbed valleys and, most importantly, large oases. The capital city, Riyadh, is located here and takes its name—*Riyadh* in Arabic means "the Gardens"—from one of the many palm plantations and fertile zones which dot the desert plain of the Najd. Dates and other fruits are grown here and throughout history there has been sufficient grazing to support the nomadic tribes of the Najd who wandered among the scattered oases.

As elsewhere in Saudi Arabia, even the slightest rainfall produces sudden growths in vegetation. For the wandering Bedouin, this dramatic appearance of pasture from the normally barren desert is a life-giving source of food for their flocks of goats, sheep and camels. Hardy plants, such as tamarisk, acacia and cactus, survive in the hot sands and rocks by such tactics as storing tiny amounts of rainwater in their roots or else by adapting and accepting salty water.

On the Arabian Gulf side of the Najd is found Hasa, the

eastern region. Compared to the drama of other parts of Saudi Arabia, this land seems almost featureless. Low hills, stony plains and scrubland stretch to the salt marshes and shallow waters of the Gulf. Much of the Gulf coastline is made up of sandflats and has little of the magnificent coral splendour of the Red Sea. Beneath all this deceptively uninteresting landscape, however, lies the source of Saudi Arabia's great wealth and prosperity—oil. And it is in this region that the great oil cities of Dammam and Dhahran are to be found with their international communities servicing the oil industry.

As well as oil, Saudi Arabia is fortunate to have other mineral deposits—phosphates, magnesium, silver, gypsum, copper, zinc and iron are now being developed. These minerals will be used in construction, industry and agriculture. Gold is also being mined near Medina, in the western region. The source is an ancient gold-mine called Mahad al Dhahab, which means "Cradle of Gold" in Arabic. According to legend, the mine was also used in the days of King Solomon.

This, then, is Saudi Arabia. A dramatic landscape of contrasts—of high mountains with cool breezes; of burning deserts; of farming villages in wet, green, terraced hills and endless windswept dusty plains; of settled townships and holy cities; and of the ever-wandering Bedouin.

Islam: The Basis of Saudi Arabian Life

For all visitors to Saudi Arabia, the most distinctive sound is the voice of the muezzin in the minaret calling the faithful to prayer: "God is most great. I testify that there is no God but God and that Muhammad is His Prophet. Come to prayer. Come to salvation. God is most great. There is no God but God." Five times a day these simple words are called out from the mosques; and five times a day the faithful pray. Islam is the most important element in Saudi Arabian life. The kingdom is the historical heart of Islam and the land of the holy cities. Mecca, the Prophet Muhammad's birthplace, and Medina both lie in the western region. It is impossible to try and understand Saudi Arabia without first trying to comprehend Islam. The two are inextricably bound together, and the history, culture, constitution and legal system of the country are firmly rooted in Islam. Even the national flag of Saudi Arabia bears an Arabic inscription which reads: "There is no God but God and Muhammad is His Prophet". It is apt that this should be on

Muslims at prayer in Mecca, the holy city of Islam

the flag for it is the *Shahada,* the Muslim profession of faith.

The word *Islam,* in Arabic, means "submission" and to be a Muslim is to be one who submits to the will of God. Muslims believe that Muhammad is the final messenger or prophet of God and that God's message, recorded and written down in the holy book known as the Quran, is the direct word of God as spoken to Muhammad in Mecca and Medina. In Arabic, *Quran* means "recitation": there are no intermediaries such as evangelists or gospel-writers. The Quran is considered to be the final, pure and perfect revelation. Muslims acknowledge that there were other prophets and revelations before Muhammad and that Allah (their name for God) is the same as the God of the Jews and the Christians. Abraham, Isaac, Moses, Joseph,

John the Baptist and Jesus are all accorded the status of being prophets of God. The Jews and the Christians are described in the Quran as "People of the Book"; that is, people who have received the word of God. It is the fact that the Quran is considered the final and complete word of God that makes it so special to Muslims. And the belief that Arabic was the language God chose for that final revelation makes it doubly special to the people of Arabia.

The essence of God's message was that the people should stop worshipping stone idols and false gods and instead turn to the one, true God and obey Holy Law. This law covered the social, moral and religious responsibilities of all believers.

All Muslims have certain religious duties. The most important are called the Five Pillars of Islam. The first of these is the *Shahada,* the profession of faith by which Muslims acknowledge their allegiance to God and His Prophet. The second pillar of Islam is *Salat,* or prayer: a Muslim must turn towards Mecca and recite the prescribed prayers five times a day. These prayers are said at dawn, midday, mid-afternoon, sunset and nightfall. For many visitors to Islamic countries, it is often surprising to see Muslims stop whatever they are doing and pray—whether they go to a mosque, or pray at their workplace, or in the street, or at home, or even in the open desert. The third pillar is the giving of alms or charity to the poor and needy. This is called *Zakat* and is an example of the social obligations involved in being a Muslim.

The fourth pillar of Islam is fasting. Every year during the entire holy month of Ramadan, Muslims abstain from eating, drinking and smoking during the daylight hours. This can be very arduous, especially in a hot climate from dawn to dusk, and the Quran makes exceptions for travellers, pregnant women, old people and the sick.

The final pillar is the *Hajj*, the pilgrimage to Mecca. Mecca is the focus of faith for millions of Muslims all over the world and it is their duty, once in their life, to perform the pilgrimage if they are fit enough and can afford it. The *Hajj* takes place at a special time each year and pilgrims from all over the world pour into Mecca. For Saudi Arabians nowadays, the pilgrimage journey is relatively easy, but it is a testament to the strength of Islam that nearly two million pilgrims, both rich and poor, come from all over the world each year and make their often long and difficult journeys by means of every form of transport known to man. They come from China, India, Pakistan, Indonesia, Nigeria, Europe, Egypt, Afghanistan and many, many more countries. There are no social distinctions on the pilgrimage: all the male pilgrims must wear identical simple white robes. It is impossible to identify a man's background or status. Muslims believe that in the eyes of God, all men are equal; the pilgrims' robes are a symbol of this.

The performing of the *Hajj* is often the high point of a Muslim's life. It brings the joy of having visited the Prophet's birthplace and of having prayed in the Holy Mosque at Mecca. Similarly, the end of Ramadan and the completion of the month of fasting is a cause for joy and celebration. At the end of the

Malaysian pilgrims dressed in their white pilgrims' robes

month the fast is broken and the holiday of Eid al Fitr begins. It is usually a holiday in all Islamic countries—a time for visiting, feasting, exchanging presents and other festive activities.

While Islam shares many things with Christianity and Judaism, such as common prophets and traditions, and the basic principles of justice, compassion, love and honesty, it differs in other ways. For Muslims, religion and life are not only indistinguishable, they are one and the same thing. Islam plays a central part in the daily life and actions of a Muslim. The

Quran contains rules and guidelines on all activities and forms of behaviour. Even the most simple acts of daily life, such as eating and drinking, are commented upon in great detail in the Quran. Trading, commerce and all dealings with money are similarly governed by clear and exact statements. While the Christian Bible and the Jewish Torah also offer rules and guidelines, neither is as detailed and extensive as the Quran. Indeed, the Quran offers to Muslims a clear definition of how they should order their social, economic and spiritual lives.

In addition to the Quran, Muslims draw upon scripts called the *Sunna,* which means "the way", or path, of the Prophet Muhammad. Contained in the *Sunna,* are the *Hadith* which means "traditions", or the words and actions of the Prophet as remembered by his followers. The law of Islam, known as the *Sharia,* is largely based on the Quran and the *Sunna.* It is from these sources that Muslim scholars find answers and interpretations to solve legal problems. In Muslim law, as in the West, the accused is considered innocent until proved guilty and the burden of proof lies with the accusers.

Many of the detailed laws governing daily life are drawn from these sources. For instance, Islam, like Judaism, prohibits the eating of all pork. Similarly, there are very strict rules governing the method of slaughtering animals for meat. Alcohol is totally forbidden and, while it is possible to buy and drink alcohol in some other Islamic countries, in Saudi Arabia it is against the law and constitutes a serious offence. Capital punishment still exists, usually by the method of beheading and usually in a public square after the midday Friday prayers. Similarly, the cutting off of hands for acts of repeated theft still exists. While these punishments may shock people in the western world, Muslims in Saudi Arabia are quick and proud to point out the relatively crime-free nature of life in their country. Any visitor to Saudi Arabia finds that this is undoubtedly true.

One common belief in the western world is that women are inferior subjects in an Islamic state. For instance, the Quran permits the practice of polygamy (having more than one wife); the limit is four. In reality, the vast majority of Saudis are monogamous—have only one wife. Women are called upon by the Quran to dress and behave with extreme modesty. Muslims see this as a symbol of the importance of women as mothers and guardians of the family. While the relative freedom of women in Islam is open to debate, it is undoubtedly true that with the advent of Muhammad and the authority of God's revealed word in the Quran, the lot of women in Arabia improved. Prior to Islam, women were virtually slaves, mere property, with no legal rights whatsoever. The Quran introduced laws of property, inheritance and divorce and, at the time, vastly improved the position of women.

The Muslim scholars in Saudi Arabia who interpret the laws are known as the Ulama. In this century they have had to pass judgement on the acceptability of many elements of modern life: television, football, the education of women and other things have all been subject to religious discussion. While television is permitted, cinemas are not. For a new country like Saudi

Arabia, emerging from centuries of unchanging isolation, the sudden headlong invasion of the modern world presents many problems. In the same way that the simple aspects of life are governed by Islamic belief, so too are the complex ones. Islam is slowly having to adapt now to the changing circumstances of twentieth-century life.

As in Christianity, there are divisions within Islam. The vast majority of Saudi Arabians are Sunni Muslims (from *Sunna*—the path of the Prophet) which means orthodox Muslims. The other group, largely restricted to the eastern oil provinces, are Shia Muslims. Sunnis and Shias differ mostly over historical points. After the Prophet Muhammad died, his successors as leaders of the Islamic community were known as caliphs or imams. The Sunnis and Shias dispute the line of succession.

For a visitor to Saudi Arabia, the evidence of Islam is everywhere. The skylines of cities, towns and villages are punctuated by the tall minarets of countless mosques. Although it is not necessary for Muslims to pray in a mosque, many do, especially on Friday, the rest day. Mosques are unlike other places of worship in that there is no altar. The interior of the mosque is largely an open space covered in carpets and prayer rugs. A niche in the wall indicates the direction of Mecca. There is usually a separate part for women. Before entering a mosque, Muslims take off their shoes and wash their face, hands and feet. This is both a sign of humility and because a state of cleanliness is considered essential for prayer.

For Muslims, then, Islam is more than an abstract set of

A mosque in Jeddah, with its slender minaret

religious beliefs: it is a total way of life. In addition to offering a spiritual path through life, it also offers a practical path to help with social, economic and political problems. And it offers, like all religions, a sense of community with other believers. In Saudi Arabia this is perhaps more evident than in other countries. The *Hajj,* or pilgrimage to Mecca, brings together Muslims of all races, classes and colours, from all points of the globe. For Muslims, all these great differences are overcome by shared belief. Out of diversity, they see a community of the faithful.

The Historical Background

The history of modern Saudi Arabia can be precisely dated: it was on the morning of January 15, 1902, that a young prince of the Saud tribe, supported by about forty men, made a daring attack on the mud-walled oasis town of Riyadh, deep in the heart of the desert. Having killed and defeated the defending soldiers, he proclaimed that his tribe, the al-Saud, were, thanks to God, masters of Riyadh and central Arabia. The young prince was Abdul Aziz bin Abdul Rahman bin Feisal al-Saud; that is, Abdul Aziz, the son of Abdul Rahman, in turn the son of Feisal, of the House of Saud. He was known to his fellow Arabs as Abdul Aziz but more commonly, in the West, he was known by the name Ibn Saud.

At that time, Arabia was a term used by Europeans to describe the entire peninsula, a name that conjured up vast and unknown deserts. There were no borders and no recognized states: it was a forgotten world, little changed since before Biblical times. Within thirty years, by war, by cunning and by statesmanship, the young prince, Ibn Saud, was to become king of a giant land stretching from the Arabian Gulf in the east to the Red Sea in the west. In later years he would preside over the discovery of "black gold"—oil, that would transform his desert kingdom into one of the richest states on earth. He was the father of modern Saudi Arabia.

Before these momentous times, however, the history of Arabia includes peoples and events going back thousands of years. It is quite difficult to piece together an accurate picture of what happened in Arabia long ago. There were very few contacts with the outside world and the desert sands have obliterated many traces of distant civilizations. Some things, however, are known. And some things, in spite of the ever-changing desert, remain.

These carvings, on ruins near Najran, are evidence that the area has been inhabited for several thousand years

Archaeologists have discovered evidence that people who inhabited the coast of the Arabian Gulf as far back as 3000 B.C. sailed great distances and traded with people and cultures as far away as India. In the centuries dating from 500 B.C. to A.D. 300 a race called the Nabataeans settled in the western part of Arabia, near to present-day Medina. They became rich by offering protection to and collecting toll money from the caravans which travelled the trade routes from the ports of Yemen in the south to the Mediterranean lands in the north. The Nabataeans built a city called Madain Saleh. Some of it can still be seen today. They carved their buildings out of rock, out of cliff faces and out of mountainsides. These were not just caves, however, but were magnificent structures: treasuries, palaces, temples and theatres.

Most ancient history in Saudi Arabia, especially in the western region, was a consequence of the overland trade routes. Southern Arabia (now the Yemen Arab Republic and the People's Democratic Republic of Yemen) was a source of silk and spices from India and of frankincense and myrrh which were used by Romans and Egyptians for various religious purposes as well as for cosmetics. The ancient Egyptians used frankincense and myrrh in the science of embalming—preserving the bodies of the dead. The mummies in our museums today are a result of this. The important commodities carried on these caravan routes were Indian silk and spices; ivory, animal skins and slaves from Africa; and gold and precious stones from Arabia itself.

A network of important caravan routes crossed the peninsula

The rock ruins of Madain Saleh, a magnificent city built by the Nabataeans some two thousand years ago

leading to Egypt, Palestine, Syria and ancient Babylon. The early inhabitants of Saudi Arabia were the middlemen in this commercial link. Towns and settlements developed along the route, and businesses grew to supply the caravans with food, water, shelter, clothing and other provisions. Protection was given against desert bandits and raiders. Many of these townships became the cities we know today, particularly Mecca and Medina. As a basis for a long-term civilization, however, it was weak. The trade routes were liable to change as the power and politics of the region changed. When the routes were no longer used, the towns and settlements decayed. The sands of the desert covered the tracks: only the magnificent rock ruins of Madain Saleh remain.

The next great phase in the history of Arabia was the birth of Islam. In the sixth century A.D., the Prophet Muhammad was born in Mecca. Even at this time Mecca was a holy city. Pagan gods and idols were worshipped, and a black stone (a meteorite which had fallen from the sky) was an object of pilgrimage. The commerce and trade of Mecca, even in those days, was largely dependent upon pilgrims. In due course, Islam grew and established itself and, in the century after Muhammad's death in A.D. 632, Arab armies stormed out of Arabia carrying the message of God and conquering lands to all points of the compass. Islam became an empire, stretching

This section from a fifteenth-century scroll, now in the British Library, depicts the sanctuary of the Ka'aba and certifies that Maymunah, daughter of Muhammad ibn Ab Allah al-Zardali, made the pilgrimage to Mecca in 1432

from Spain in the west to India and central Asia in the east. Despite these great conquests, this great flowering of Arab and Islamic civilization, the changes in Arabia itself were not dramatic. The capital of the Islamic empire was in Damascus, in Syria, because of its more advanced culture and its more central geographical position.

New trade routes opened elsewhere in the new empire. In Arabia, only the holy cities and a few small ports for pilgrims prospered. Much of the rest of Arabia was as ever: lawless desert wastes. For nearly a thousand years, Arabia remained a place of mystery. In the sixteenth century the Turks of the Ottoman Empire occupied key parts of the country and Arabia fell under the sway of Turkish influence. Even then, it remained a forbidding and unknown world.

For Europeans in the age of the explorers it was an extremely difficult country to visit. The climate, language and customs were hard to master. Entrance to the holy cities was, and still is, strictly forbidden to non-Muslims. Even so, several explorers, disguised as Muslim pilgrims, penetrated the deserts and holy places and brought back maps and descriptions. But they were few in number. It was not until after Ibn Saud's attack on Riyadh that Arabia was to become more open to the world at large.

One other key event in Saudi Arabia's history occurred in the eighteenth century. A religious reformer, Abdul Wahhab, made a treaty with Muhammad Ibn Saud, an ancestor of Abdul Aziz Ibn Saud and of today's royal family. Abdul Wahhab had seen a slow decay in Islam as a religion and even a return to the old desert ways of worshipping stones and idols. He resolved to re-establish a pure religion based on Islam as it was at the time of the Prophet Muhammad. His religious outlook was very puritan and strict. With the help of the al-Saud tribe, he proclaimed the return to this pure religion. Converts flocked to his call and soon the central region, the Najd, was the focus of an attempt to unify the tribes and the land under a pure and strict Islam. Gradually, the rule of the al-Saud tribe grew and expanded eastwards and westwards. The Turks of the Ottoman Empire disliked this new power in central Arabia and, slowly, the power of the al-Saud, and with it the strict Islam of Wahhab, began to be eroded.

Towards the end of the nineteenth century, another tribe, the al-Rashid, fought for supremacy in central Arabia and the al-Saud escaped into exile in the northern deserts and in what is now Kuwait. Once again, Arabia was a desert land of disunited tribes. It was from Kuwait that the young prince, Abdul Aziz Ibn Saud, was to march with his forty men and his camels to recapture Riyadh from the al-Rashid and again proclaim the return to a pure Islam. It was from this small beginning in 1902 that modern Saudi Arabia was to grow.

Modern Saudi Arabia

The Arabia of 1902 in which Ibn Saud began his rise to power had changed little in over a thousand years. The surrounding deserts were still the home of clans and tribes who cared only for their own honour and were loyal only unto themselves. The years which followed immediately after the taking of Riyadh were years of constant fighting. The Turks supported the al-Rashid and other tribes against the new masters of Riyadh. Ibn Saud's aim was to establish a disciplined society, with his own central authority based upon the law of the Quran. To do this he had to use his Bedouin army to break the resistance of the unruly tribes. He formed communities of hard, and some say fanatic, soldiers. They were called the Ikhwan (literally, "the Brothers") and they became the spearhead of his attempt to impose discipline and religious authority. The Ikhwan were fierce and greatly feared in battle. They believed their war was a holy crusade and that to die in battle guaranteed passage to heaven. Their military strength was crucial in Ibn Saud's early battles and in his later expansion into other parts of Arabia. Their strength and religious zeal were, however, to cause him problems in later years.

By 1914 Ibn Saud had conquered most of central Arabia and the eastern province. He was recognized as Emir or Prince of the Najd. During the First World War (1914 – 1918), the Ottoman Empire began to collapse and the Turks lost ground throughout the Middle East. At this time, the western region, the Hejaz, was ruled separately by a rival of Ibn Saud's named Hussein. The famous English adventurer and soldier, Lawrence of Arabia, helped Hussein and the tribes of the Hejaz to revolt against Turkish domination, with the British promise of Arabian independence after the war. The Turks were duly defeated and Hussein proclaimed himself King of the Hejaz. Inevitably, Hussein and Ibn Saud were drawn into conflict. By 1925, after years of fighting, Ibn Saud defeated Hussein and became the new King of the Hejaz.

In the following years, Ibn Saud had to turn his energies towards the defeat of his own shock troops, the Ikhwan, who had become uncontrollable. By now, the ferocity of the Ikhwan had become notorious. Permanently dissatisfied and thirsting for war, they threatened the stability of Ibn Saud's new authority. In 1929 Ibn Saud raised a Bedouin army and finally crushed the Ikhwan in what was to be the last great desert battle in Arabia.

In September 1932, Ibn Saud proclaimed the creation of the Kingdom of Saudi Arabia, using his own family name to describe the lands under his authority. In Arabic, the name of the country is simply Saudia.

King Abdul Aziz Ibn Saud was then fifty-two years old and the undisputed ruler of a land which was experiencing a form of unity for the first time in its history. He was renowned for his fairness in disputes. His imposing figure (he was extremely tall by Bedouin standards) dominated tribal divisions. From the beginning he established a firm rule, with strictly enforced laws. He guaranteed the safety of pilgrims to the Holy Cities of Mecca and Medina, and his power was unchallenged from the Arabian Gulf to the Red Sea. The British Government, then the major foreign power in Middle East politics, recognized his authority. The port city of Jeddah soon became the home of a number of foreign consuls. But the new kingdom was a poor country. After years of internal war, there was little or no trade. The only revenue came from the pilgrim trade. Outside Saudi Arabia, the world was experiencing the great Depression of the 1930s and the new kingdom also suffered as a result.

Throughout the years since the capture of Riyadh in 1902, Ibn Saud had extended his influence and power and helped to unify tribes by intermarriage. Under Islam, a man is allowed a maximum of four wives at any time. Ibn Saud did not exceed this limit, but he regularly exercised his right of divorce and throughout his life had numerous wives, perhaps over a hundred. These marriages, many of them for political reasons, led to an extended network, a vast family tree. While the scale of Ibn Saud's marriages and the number of his children, said

A portrait of Abdul Aziz Ibn Saud, the founder of the modern state of Saudi Arabia

to number hundreds, may seem surprising, the basic principles are similar to marriage conventions elsewhere. In Europe it was often the practice of royal families to inter-marry, both as a means of unifying peoples and of achieving national aims. In the same way, Ibn Saud married into the important tribes of Arabia and thus strengthened his influence through family ties. In a greater sense, these were also the ties that helped to bind his kingdom together. Today, the size of the al-Saud family is not known exactly but it is measured in thousands. There is no doubt that much of the stability of Saudi Arabia stems from this wide distribution of power and influence.

In the early 1930s an event occurred which was to have far-reaching and dramatic consequences for the struggling kingdom and ultimately for the world. In his need for money, Ibn Saud sold concessions for oil exploration. (A concession is a legal permit to search for oil in a particular area.) For several years, British and American oil companies had believed there was oil below the barren desert. Oil had already been discovered in southern Iraq and what is now Iran, as well as in the island of Bahrain, just off Saudi Arabia's eastern coast. In 1933 the King permitted an American company to explore. By 1938 the first important oil wells were gushing in the eastern province near modern-day Dhahran. Ibn Saud, whose youthful kingdom had only just been saved from bankruptcy by the money given for the oil concession, could now face a brighter future.

By 1939 oil production had started. During the Second World War (1939 – 1945), the Trans Arabian Pipeline was built. It stretched for 1,700 kilometres (over 1,000 miles), from the Arabian Gulf across the desert to the Mediterranean port of Sidon in Lebanon. The stage was now set for the economic miracle which would transform the poor kingdom.

At first the much needed revenues from the oil came slowly and a lot of money was wasted. This was inevitable in a society which was unused to managing its economy. Gradually, plans for road-building and house-building emerged. The modern world began to invade the desert kingdom. Thirty years before, Ibn Saud and his warriors had crossed the seemingly endless deserts by camel. Now, flying in an airliner which was a gift from the United States President Roosevelt, he toured his kingdom and visited outposts, tribal meetings, oil wells and scattered towns. With the help of the American airline T.W.A., Saudi Arabian Airlines, later to become Saudia, was set up as the national civil airline. Plans were drawn up to develop education and health care. New schools and hospitals were built. Slowly, from almost nothing, and in the space of a few years, the foundations of a modern state were being laid.

Ibn Saud died in 1953 in the mountain city of Taif. As was the custom, he was buried the same day in an unmarked grave in Riyadh, the city whose capture in 1902 had been the first step towards nationhood. He was succeeded by his eldest son, Saud. There followed a difficult period for the nation. Ibn Saud had lived an austere life, a life of relative poverty and simplicity. Now, the plentiful and easy money pouring into the kingdom as oil revenues proved difficult to handle for his son, the new king. The economy was badly mismanaged.

At the same time, throughout the Arab world there was a new spirit—a spirit of nationalism, of republicanism and of revolution. The source of this new ideology was Cairo and its voice was Gamal Abdul Nasser, the Egyptian President. His ideas and speeches were broadcast all over the Middle East by Radio Cairo—the ''Voice of the Arabs''—and his attacks against conservative monarchies and royal families shook the whole Arab world. Nasser had come to power in the period following the military overthrow of King Farouk of Egypt in 1952. Elsewhere in the Middle East, the old order of monarchs and titled leaders seemed to be tumbling. To the Saudi monarchy (tribal, conservative and religious) this message of revolution was dangerous. The Saudi rulers were in a difficult position between slowly modernizing their strict society and satisfying those who wanted reforms and changes at a faster pace.

To the south of the country, in the Yemen, a group of army officers deposed the Imam, the ruler, and seized power. Slowly the countries surrounding Saudi Arabia were being turned into republics. Civil war followed in the Yemen, with Saudi Arabia backing the royalists and Egypt supporting the republicans. Eventually, the war came to an end in 1967 when Egypt could no longer afford to keep up this support. By that time, Feisal had taken over as King of Saudi Arabia and it seemed that the nation had survived the crisis.

It was during the period of Feisal's reign that the first major plans for present-day Saudi Arabia were laid. Feisal recognized that, despite the deeply Islamic nature of his kingdom, the ideal way for it to make progress was to absorb the best of western technology while preserving Islamic values.

His development plans were designed to guarantee these values while building up the economy, making education and health care freely available, increasing communications and transport networks and, perhaps most importantly, decreasing the dependence upon oil. This was all to be done gradually, by using oil revenues wisely, and by setting up other local and national industries. A major problem of the new kingdom was its need to import nearly everything from abroad: cars, trucks, machines and tools, foodstuffs, plastics, building materials and medicines. In the long term, Saudi Arabia aimed to be self-sufficient in some of these areas—to produce enough to meet its own needs and, if possible, even become an exporter of some of these products.

Two wars, between Israel and Arab countries led by Egypt, dominated the years of King Feisal's reign. The Arab defeat of 1967 was partially balanced by the events of 1973 which were considered a political victory for the Arab states. It was in 1973 and 1974 that Saudi Arabia first employed what came to be known as the "oil weapon". Because oil is so important to the advanced western countries, and to the running of industry, any cut in production or increase in prices can have a devastating effect. The Saudis, and other Arab oil-producing nations, used this economic weapon in an effort to make the United States and other countries stop supplying Israel with military equipment. They also wanted to bring international pressure to bear upon Israel in an attempt to make the Israelis withdraw from the city of Jerusalem and other lands which had been taken and occupied during the war. Jerusalem is a holy city for Jews, Christians and Muslims. The Israeli occupation of the holy city in 1967 shocked all Muslims, as does the continued homelessness of the Palestinian people.

Because of its vast wealth, Saudi Arabia now has a great

Placards carrying the portraits of members of the Saudi royal family, direct descendants of Ibn Saud who first united the country in the early twentieth century

influence on the politics and economics of the Middle East and beyond. A continuing major concern of Saudi policy has been the seeking of a solution to the Arab–Israeli conflict and the Palestinian problem.

Modern-day Saudi Arabia is aware of the responsibilities, both national and international, that its wealth has brought. In recent years, it has assumed a greater role in both the Middle East region and the developing world. Today, Saudi Arabia is ruled by King Fahd who succeeded his brother Khalid (who died in 1982). King Khalid had succeeded Feisal, who was assassinated in 1975. The country is a monarchy with the Quran as the constitution. The King is both the chief of state and the head of a government in which he is assisted by a Council of Ministers. There are no political parties and no elections. In addition, while there is no representative government in the western sense, there is a strong policy of equality in the eyes of the law. Individual freedoms and the rights of grievance and complaint are embodied in the law derived from the Quran. Despite the rapid modernization, Saudi Arabia is still essentially conservative and religious. Considering the impact of massive wealth on such a traditional and isolated people, and considering also the deep belief in Islam, it is hardly surprising that progress and reform are cautious.

The Bedouin

Far from the modern cities and industrial complexes of Saudi Arabia, deep in the desert, people live in long black tents made from goat-hair. Near to the tents will be a few camels, or a small flock of sheep or goats. The only visible concession to the modern world may be a jeep or a pick-up truck. These people are the Bedouin. In days gone by, most of the desert zones were the province of great Bedouin tribes. Today, the majority of Saudi citizens claim Bedouin ancestry. Even in the western region of the Hejaz, with its history of settled communities and racial intermingling, the people still turn to the traditions of honour and hospitality of the Bedouin. To understand much of the Saudi Arabian character, it is necessary first to understand the traditions and character of the Bedouin.

The Bedouin are nomads—wanderers, people of no fixed abode. Historically, they have lived lives of constant movement, ever searching for pasture for their flocks. It is thought that the word "Arab" and the word "Hebrew", come from the same root and mean "wanderer". In Arabia, even in ancient times, the Bedouin were outnumbered by settled peoples. The eastern coastal regions were occupied by fishing and pearl-diving communities and the western region by merchants, farmers and people who made a living off the caravan and pilgrim trades. But it is in the character of the Bedouin that most of the attitudes and patterns of Arabian life are to be found.

The environment in which the Bedouin lived shaped their character and their traditions. The desert was hostile and inhospitable. Wandering for most of the year, dependent on their camels and living on the edge of existence, the Bedouin were hard people and the code by which they lived was a code of survival, first and foremost. The family was the foundation of all Bedouin society and, after that, came the tribe. Raids on other tribes were a common feature of life, but even these were subject to certain codes of honour. The object of a raid was to steal the camels belonging to other tribes, not to steal personal property or to injure life. In the fickle world of the desert, family and tribal fortunes changed suddenly, and the raiders of today knew only too well that they themselves could be the victims of tomorrow's raid.

The key traditions of the Bedouin were concerned with family honour, loyalty and hospitality. Dignity was also highly valued and any injury or insult to a Bedouin was avenged. The rule of the desert was "an eye for an eye". Sometimes an individual, or a family, carried out the act of revenge; and sometimes vengeance was taken by an entire tribe. Disputes and blood feuds could last for years, between individuals, families or tribes.

At the same time, in contrast to the raids and the acts of

A Bedouin woman at work in a traditional outdoor kitchen

revenge, the Bedouin are renowned to this day for their hospitality. The reason behind their open generosity and hospitality lies in the fact that to refuse strangers food, water or shelter in the harsh world of the desert was to condemn them to almost certain death. The tradition was, and indeed still is, that by kissing or touching the hem of a Bedouin tent, a stranger is guaranteed three days of hospitality, even if he is an enemy. This "chivalry" was born out of the hard and perilous life of the desert nomad and the awareness that everyone is in need of help at some point.

Another curious aspect of Bedouin existence was that life was relatively democratic within the tribes. Because there was very little wealth and little in the way of material possessions, there were few social distinctions: even the plunder from raids was shared out. There were rulers—*sheikhs,* literally "old men"—tribal seniors who were respected for their age, wisdom and experience, but they lived exactly as the others did and ate from the same communal plates of rice. These *sheikhs* or elders of the tribe would meet and discuss all matters of tribal, family or individual importance. Regular meetings and councils took place: these were known as *majlis* and they are still a feature of Saudi life at all levels. Even the Kings of Saudi Arabia have held open court and any citizen can come and air grievances or discuss problems. Indeed, the King and other royal princes travel the length and breadth of the kingdom, meeting and consulting with different tribes.

Bedouin men drinking tea

Another aspect of Bedouin tradition which has affected modern Arabian life dramatically is the sense of kinship within families. Marriages were often arranged within the tribe; and it was not uncommon for a man to marry his first cousin, or for uncles to marry nieces, or nephews to marry aunts. This created a very close-knit family and tribal structure.

Bedouin society was polygamous (each man was allowed more than one wife at a time) and so large families developed. The ties created by marriages led to complex family trees and helped to cement unity both within a tribe and between different tribes. Often the purpose of a particular marriage was to create a bond between tribes, to gain influence or to gain protection from a stronger tribe. The Bedouin married from an early age. Girls of twelve or thirteen became brides, sometimes to elderly men—the *sheikhs* of the tribe.

Today, this sense of kinship is reflected in the close ties which still dominate family life in Saudi Arabia. Any visitor to the country, and indeed to much of the Arab world, notices the respect given to older members of the family and the easy mixing of grandparents, children and grandchildren in the same family. Much of the architecture of Arabian homes reveals the importance given to this extended family. Traditional Arab houses are large, with a central, secluded courtyard. They have women's quarters (the harem) and men's quarters. Several generations may be found in the one family home. Families are usually large and everyone, from the oldest to the youngest, has a role to play. This strong family bond was born out of the need for security and support in the harsh isolation of the desert. Even today in the cities and the towns, it gives many Saudi Arabians a sense of community. And it is this sense of family identity which forms the foundation of Saudi society.

The life of the Bedouin, then, was largely one of wandering in search of grazing for their flocks. Raids on other tribes provided a diversion from what was often a monotonous life. They also gave the Bedouin the chance of increasing their camel herds and flocks, thereby increasing their prosperity. The raids also provided subjects for story-telling and poetry, skills much prized in the long desert nights.

Bedouin women are also still renowned for their weaving. Traditionally the wool came from the camels, goats and sheep. The women wove tents, rugs, cushions, clothes and saddle-bags, using dyes, such as indigo, made from local plants. The life of the Bedouin women was hard—bearing and rearing their children, cooking, weaving, pitching tents and striking camp and sometimes helping with the shepherding of flocks. The women prepared and cooked simple food: traditional Bedouin food consists of dates and yoghurt, roast meat and rice. The meat was invariably tough and usually from one of the old sheep, goats or camels. On special days and celebrations, the meat of a young lamb or camel would be roasted. Ground coffee, spiced with cardamom seeds, was the common drink. Often the roast meat, perhaps an entire sheep, would be served on a large bed of rice and everyone would eat together, taking handfuls from the same plate.

A young Bedouin girl, with a typical woven rug in the background

Without the camel, the special life of the Bedouin would not have been possible. The camel of Arabia is a single-humped dromedary and is capable of storing huge reserves of water for days on end and enduring the hottest and most difficult of environments. The camel can be an extremely bad-tempered animal and difficult to handle, but it provided the Bedouin with many things that made life possible and bearable: transport, milk, hair for weaving, meat. Even dried camel dung had its uses: it was the basis of a good campfire. It was also used as the pieces in a Bedouin game similar to draughts.

With the advent of wealth and prosperity to Saudi Arabia, the old Bedouin pattern of life has changed. Highways and oil pipelines now criss-cross the desert, and jets reduce to a matter of hours journeys which once took weeks. The Bedouin, always outnumbered by village and townspeople, are now a tiny minority. Some still wander the desert, living a life which has been almost unchanged for nearly three thousand years. Others have moved to the new towns and cities and settled into urban life. The Bedouin, while never entirely representative of Arabian life, are nevertheless the root of Saudi Arabian culture.

The People Today: Daily Life in Saudi Arabia

The majority of people in Saudi Arabia today live in modern cities, towns and villages. Within one extended family, the ages may range from grandparents in their eighties or nineties to newborn babies. Within such a family, therefore, may be found the whole experience of modern Saudi Arabia. The grandparents may remember their own childhood before Saudi Arabia even existed as a unified nation: a childhood very different to that of their grandchildren and great-grandchildren now. It was a slow world of hardship and poverty, but one enriched by traditions and legends. The child of today, by contrast, is born into a world of sophisticated hospitals, mass education, highways and airports, and supermarkets with shelves full of the world's best produce. The grandparents' world was almost static, unchanged for over a thousand years; for the grandchildren, life in modern Saudi Arabia reflects constant and dynamic change.

In recent years, in the cities, such as Jeddah, Riyadh and

Saudi children in Jeddah Old Town—their lives are very different from those of their grandparents

Dammam, Saudi citizens could almost feel outnumbered. Foreigners—other Arabs, Europeans, Americans and people from the Far East—have come in their hundreds of thousands to work in Saudi Arabia. Port cities, such as Jeddah, and the pilgrim cities of Mecca and Medina, have always been relatively cosmopolitan—full of people from other parts of the world—but these were mostly Muslim or Arabic-speaking people. By contrast, the recent huge influx of people and commodities from the four corners of the world has been the most marked change in Saudi society.

A young Saudi man today may drive to work in an American

car, wearing a Swiss watch and clothes tailored in Pakistan or Hong Kong. At work, he may speak English to his colleagues who may well be a mixture comprising Europeans, fellow Muslims from other Arab countries, Americans and Koreans. Even the street names and road signs are written in English and Arabic. In the evening he may go to a restaurant and eat pizza or an American beefburger, before returning home to watch a European football match on his Japanese television set. He belongs to modern Saudi Arabia which is open to the world; his grandfather belonged to a closed world.

Foreign visitors are often surprised when they go to Saudi Arabia. They arrive and find a country which, in many ways, is more modern and sophisticated than the one they left behind. The two largest and most modern airports in the world are in Jeddah and Riyadh. From them the visitor drives down eight-lane highways into cities full of skyscrapers, modern high-rise office blocks and neon signs. Below the surface of all this modernity, however, many aspects of Saudi life are still traditional. And while the young Saudi man at work may live and work in a sea of foreign people, foreign goods and foreign influences, it is in the traditional world of the home and the family, and of the Muslim community, that he lives most of his life.

A Saudi family today is as likely to live in a tower-block apartment as in a traditional home with its central courtyard and women's and men's quarters. Wherever Saudis live, eating together with family or friends is a regular social occasion for

A view of the centre of cosmopolitan Jeddah, with its modern skyscrapers and office blocks

them. And, while there are many places in which to buy or eat foreign foods, most Saudis more commonly eat traditional food. It is difficult to talk of Saudi Arabian food since there are so many influences from neighbouring Arab countries. The most traditional meal is the old Bedouin one of roast meat served on a bed of rice, flavoured with herbs and spices, and eaten communally. In the coastal areas, fish is very popular, accompanied by rice, salad and bread. Bread is eaten with nearly every meal—the flat circular bread which is common throughout the entire Arab world. Chicken, with a soup-like mixture of tomato sauce and vegetables, is also popular. Dates are common

A group of Saudi men eating lamb and rice in the traditional manner

everywhere and still form part of the staple diet, whether eaten as a dessert or taken with coffee. Other popular sweets include *baklava*, a sticky mixture of syrup, honey and nuts. And, of course, there is coffee. The origins of coffee are not known, but one theory is that coffee was first grown in southern Arabia, near what is now the port of Mocha in North Yemen. For thousands of years it has been the traditional Arabian drink. It is made and served with great ritual and ceremony. Coffee beans are first roasted, then ground and boiled with cardamom seeds and sugar. The drink produced is strongly flavoured and served in small cups.

Other foods are also very popular and can be found in hundreds of small take-away restaurants and cafés. They include *falafel*, deep fried balls of ground chickpeas and herbs; *shawarma*, a sandwich of roast meat and pickled vegetables; *hummous,* a purée of chickpeas and oil. Many of these foods are Middle Eastern in origin rather than Saudi Arabian, but they have become the "fast food" of the country and are now part of the way of life there.

Eating is generally more than just a necessary daily activity. It is part of the social life and entertainment of Saudis. News and stories are exchanged over the course of an evening meal. It is also a re-affirmation of family togetherness and friendship.

During the day in Saudi Arabia, working hours are generally from seven in the morning through to mid-afternoon. This is fairly normal for very hot countries. Rush-hour traffic jams can occur at two o'clock in the afternoon. Some businesses and workplaces work longer hours. Indeed, one aspect of the dynamic change in Saudi Arabia is the almost constant activity with work on construction sites and road-building going on around the clock.

The workers from all parts of the world wear a variety of costumes. There are Europeans, Americans and Far Eastern workers in light clothes because of the heat; Pakistanis in baggy cotton trousers; Egyptians in long robes known as *jellabias;* and Sudanese and other Africans in brightly-coloured robes. Saudi Arabians stand out from this great crowd by virtue of their own national and traditional dress.

Saudi men wear a long flowing white robe which covers the entire body from neck to feet, with sleeves coming down to the wrists. This is called the *thobe.* To cover the head, a cotton headdress is worn, known as the *ghutra*. Usually this is of red and white checked material. But in the hotter summer months, many Saudi men wear a plain white *ghutra*. The headdress is held in place by a double black rope called the *iqal*. These clothes are simple and elegant. The loose white robes reflect the sun and allow the air to circulate; the headdress provides essential shade in the fierce sun.

Most Saudi women, by contrast, wear black. Older women are generally dressed from head to toe in black, very often with a short veil covering the hair but revealing the face. Younger women, however, may well wear modern western clothing at

A rural family in Saudi Arabia, wearing their simple and distinctive national dress

A spice stall in Riyadh's *souk*

home, but cover themselves with a silky black cloak called the *abbaya* when they go out in public.

When work is over and the sun has set, the towns and cities of Saudi Arabia are at their busiest. Whole Saudi families drive to the shopping centres and markets. The kingdom is now a rich country and even the foreign workers are relatively well-off. One result is that shopping, whether in brand new air-conditioned covered shopping plazas or in the ancient crowded traditional markets, known as *souks,* is now a major activity.

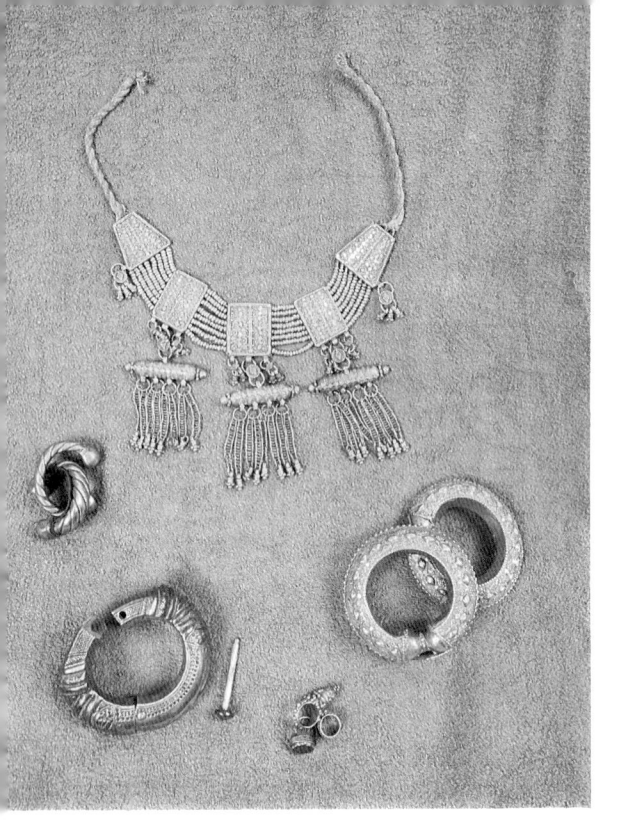

Traditional silver Bedouin jewellery such as this can be bought in Saudi Arabia's bustling *souks*

The *souks* are the noisiest, most interesting and attractive markets. They include old Arabian buildings, winding alleyways, spice stalls, old mosques, carpets and rugs from all over the East, pottery, silverware, Bedouin jewellery, copper and brass. The *souks* are a babel of languages. Noisy haggling and bargaining is still the common method of buying and selling. The *souks* still give a sense of old Arabia.

Most markets and shops stay open until after ten o'clock or even later in the evening. It is not surprising, therefore, to be in a traffic jam even at this late stage of the day. Cars are everywhere. Although the Saudis have mostly lost their beloved camels, the car has become their equally loved substitute. Driving is an important part of Saudi life nowadays—although much of it is fast and dangerous. It is also a necessity in a country where distances are great, to transport friends and families to desert picnics and to beaches; or just to cruise through the cool desert evenings. Perhaps constant movement is in the Bedouin or Arabian blood and driving provides an ideal outlet for this. For many young men particularly, driving is almost the centre of their lives. It provides all their entertainment. Women, however, are not permitted to drive in Saudi Arabia. This prohibition extends to all women, both Saudi as well as foreign.

Saudi Arabia is a very youthful nation. The majority of the population is below the age of twenty-five. It is little wonder, therefore, that nearly all forms of sport are catered for and played. The most popular is undoubtedly football. It is played everywhere from new sports stadiums to rough patches of sand and vacant carparks.

Each year, with the coming of the cooler weather, the Saudis make weekend trips to the desert, and the old Bedouin tradition of hunting with falcons is still practised. All year round, in the evenings, many Saudi men, particularly the older generation, sit in cafés, drinking coffee, playing dominoes and smoking the old traditional pipes known as *hookahs*.

Marriages are still traditionally between distant relatives of the same family or tribe and are arranged by the parents. Often the young couple see each other for the first time on their wedding day. Before any marriage is agreed upon, a dowry must be paid to the bride's family. Dowries can be extremely expensive. Nowadays, however, more and more young couples are breaking with tradition and choosing their own marriage partners.

Throughout Saudi Arabia, in the crowded cities and towns and in the isolated farming villages, the way of life is inevitably changing. There are many new activities, entertainments and distractions. Underlying everything, however, is the deep-rooted Saudi love of traditional ways—of family gatherings, communal meals, visiting friends and relatives and enjoying conversation.

Falcons ready for the hunt. Hawking is an old Bedouin tradition which is still practised in modern Saudi Arabia

Smoking *hookah* pipes in a Saudi café

The sense of family life and Muslim identity are still the strongest forces in Saudi society. In the rapidly changing world, these things remain.

The Economy: Industry and Agriculture

The foundation of Saudi Arabia's spectacular growth has been oil—the vast reservoirs of "black gold" beneath the desert sands of the eastern province. It is estimated that Saudi Arabia possesses about one quarter of the proven oil reserves in the world.

It was in 1938, after five fruitless years of searching, that American explorers first struck oil. The location was Dhahran. Soon other rich oilfields were discovered. By 1945, there was an oil industry of international importance in Saudi Arabia. The original American companies involved in the drilling and exploration had, by this time, been renamed Aramco (The Arabian American Oil Company). Aramco undertook the development of the oil industry. Vast refineries rose on Saudi Arabia's desolate eastern shore. Pipelines were laid across the desert, and deep-water tanker terminals were built in the Arabian Gulf.

In these early days, the exploration and development took

place against a backdrop of desert tribal society. The discovery of the oil led to many changes. Aramco built roads, houses, work camps, airfields and industrial complexes. American oil engineers and geologists made the first detailed maps of the region. Jobs and steady employment became available to a people who had, until then, wandered from oasis to oasis and not known regular work. Foreign workers and experts arrived. Oil did not simply bring money: it brought momentous changes to the Saudi way of life.

It is difficult, even now, to estimate the size of Saudi Arabia's oilfields; each year new oil deposits are discovered. Depending on the rate at which oil is extracted, there may be enough to last for over a hundred years. The figures relating to Saudi oil production are so vast that it is sometimes difficult to comprehend them. Present-day oil production varies in quantity in relation to oil prices and the world demand. In the early 1980s, however, the production rate was about ten million barrels per day. Saudi Arabia is the world's largest exporter of oil. Most of it is shipped by tankers to Europe, America and Japan to be refined. Some of it is also refined in Saudi Arabia, in refineries at Ras Tanura on the Gulf and Jeddah on the Red Sea. Pipelines also carry oil to Bahrain and across the Middle East to the Mediterranean countries.

It may seem surprising, but one of the main problems which the Saudi Government has had to face has been how to spend the huge amount of money earned by oil. Sometimes, despite the widespread development of Saudi society, it has not been

The Saudi Petrochemicals Company in Jubail

possible to spend all the revenues. As a result, vast reserves of surplus money accumulated. Some of this has been invested overseas, in foreign banks, property and businesses and a considerable amount has been given as foreign aid to other Islamic and developing countries.

Oil revenues have always been the main source of income for Saudi Arabia. All modern development has been oil-based. But, as for many other oil-rich countries in the region, the main problem facing Saudi Arabia has been how to reduce this dependence on oil.

In the early years nearly all the money from oil was used to finance the dramatic growth of the country. After oil, construction was the largest industry. For over thirty years, Saudi Arabia has sometimes seemed like a giant building-site. Houses, roads, schools, universities, hospitals, factories, refineries, airports and seaports have all been built from virtually nothing. Cities have witnessed spectacular growth.

Much of the early construction work was aimed at overcoming the problems of communication and survival in a hot climate and a difficult landscape. Roads and airports were an immediate necessity. Most importantly, the problem of water supply was tackled. Only between ten and fifteen per cent of the land is arable in Saudi Arabia. And the supply of fresh drinking water has been a problem since the dawn of history. Desalination plants were built—complexes that are capable of producing fresh

Building a new flyover near Mecca. After oil, construction is the largest industry in Saudi Arabia and new roads have a high priority

The huge desalination plant in Jeddah

water from the sea water of the Gulf and the Red Sea by extracting the salt. In Jeddah, the huge desalination plant produces over twenty million litres (five million gallons) of fresh water per day. Elsewhere, especially in the south-west, dams and irrigation projects were begun, to make maximum use of the rainfall in that part of the country. Also in those early years, electricity was introduced on a large scale. Diesel generating plants were built, using the plentiful local oil as fuel.

Today, the main trend in Saudi economic planning is to diversify from oil—to enter other fields of industry and build up new commercial concerns. The greatest of these new projects involves the building of two entirely new industrial cities: Jubail on the east coast and Yanbu on the west coast. This dramatic plan is based upon the use of a by-product of oil—natural gas.

In years gone by, the gas from the oilfields was flared—set alight and burned. In fact, a dramatic sight in the Middle East, especially at night, was to see the flames from the desert oilfields as the gas was fired. Now, however, this extra fuel resource is being preserved for use in setting up the new industries. In many ways, Jubail in particular seems destined to be the miracle of modern Saudi development. Situated on the shores of the Gulf, only a few years ago it had several hundred inhabitants. Within ten years it will be a city of nearly 350,000 people, with over twenty new industries, a large port, an international airport, and factories and plants. Chemicals, plastics, fertilizers, steel and aluminium will be among the things produced. It is the greatest example of Saudi Arabia's determination to build up a varied industrial economy. This will help to guarantee continued prosperity independent of oil.

Throughout the kingdom, many minerals are now mined to supply the Saudi demand, especially in connection with building materials. New Saudi-controlled companies have been created to exploit these resources. Marble, limestone, gypsum and cement are produced for the construction industry. In the mid-1970s there was a construction boom in many parts of the country. Jeddah port was so congested that ships from all over the world could not find a berth to unload their cargoes. Such was the desperate need for cement that helicopters were used to unload foreign cement from ships anchored in the Red Sea. Nowadays, nearly all the cement necessary is supplied by national companies. Allied to this new trend of self-sufficiency in building materials is the growth of large-scale Saudi construction companies. Until recently, most construction was carried out by overseas firms.

Perhaps the most surprising developments have been made in the area of agriculture. In a land which is largely barren desert, and where temperatures are extremely high and rain is scarce, huge advances have been made. The kingdom is even self-sufficient in wheat and several other crops. The most common crops are wheat, millet, barley and dates. Water supply, inevitably, has been the greatest problem. But, with the advent of desalinated water, dams and irrigation systems, a wide variety of fruit and vegetables is now grown. Experimental farms have been set up to study new agricultural methods and the possibilities of growing crops with very small amounts of water.

Overhead irrigation systems, such as this, mean that Saudi Arabia is now able to grow a wide variety of fruit and vegetables

Telecommunications — another area in which the Saudi economy has seen spectacular growth

Huge herds of dairy cattle and sheep now provide the bulk of milk, butter and cheese, where before they were almost entirely imported from overseas. Although it is expected that the kingdom will never be entirely self-sufficient in major foodstuffs, the many advances in livestock control and successful crop-growing will at least ensure that it is not wholly dependent on the outside world for its foodstuffs.

Another area of the economy which has seen spectacular growth is telecommunications. The telephone and telex have played a vital part in modern Saudi Arabia. Communications systems of all sorts are now essential to government and business efficiency. These systems have been extended to overseas and the country now enjoys excellent communications with the rest of the world. This is a striking example of the change in Saudi Arabia. Only a generation or two ago it was a closed and mysterious land. Now Riyadh is the control headquarters of the first Arab satellite, Arabsat, which was launched by the United States space shuttle. The satellite, owned and controlled by many Arab countries, further improves communications.

Two trends can therefore be seen in the Saudi Arabian economy. One is the increasing emergence of Saudi-owned and Saudi-controlled companies competing with international firms, and the other is the continued movement away from oil into the other industries. A recent example of this has been the dramatic growth of hundreds of small manufacturing concerns throughout the kingdom. These produce a whole range of goods from processed food and plastic bags to clothing and furniture. Most importantly, they create new sources of income and employment outside the oil industry.

Saudi Arabia is still growing. Thanks to the huge wealth created by oil, it has been able to avoid the difficulties and problems which face other developing countries.

The Cities and the Towns

Seventy years ago there were very few detailed maps of what is now Saudi Arabia. Around the coasts, towns and ports known to sea-going traders were marked on maps; the interior of the land, however, was mostly marked as unknown desert. The maps were often inaccurate, the result of guesswork as much as knowledge. All the maps nevertheless conveyed the immense sense of emptiness and the scarcity of substantial towns or settlements. Saudi Arabia is still a land of vast space but nowadays there are giant, sprawling cities where before there were only villages and oasis communities.

THE WESTERN REGION—THE HEJAZ

Mecca is the birthplace of the Prophet Muhammad and the spiritual centre for over 800 million people throughout the Islamic world. Five times a day, Muslims everywhere turn to this sacred city with its Holy Mosque and pray. The centre of the city is occupied by the enormous mosque which can hold about one million people. In the vast central courtyard of the mosque, overlooked by seven minarets, is the Ka'aba—the Ka'aba is a small square shrine built of stone and covered by a black cloth with the names of God woven in gold thread. In one corner of the Ka'aba, embedded in silver, is the black stone, the meteorite worshipped by pilgrims and believed to be a fragment of the original temple erected by Abraham. The Holy Mosque is always busy with pilgrims, praying and walking round the black cube of the Ka'aba in a flowing sea of white robes, some touching or kissing the black stone.

Throughout history, Mecca has been a pilgrim city and a melting-pot of different peoples. Many trades and professions flourished as a result of this. Today, Mecca is essentially the same, but bigger and more modern. It is located high in a bowl of mountains. With the advent of international air travel, the scale of the annual pilgrimage, the *Hajj*, has changed dramatically. Each year, as many as two million people converge on the city. A new airport has been built, with new highways to connect it with the Holy Mosque, other holy places and the hotels and camps necessary to house the influx of people. Mecca is a dramatic city: old Arab houses, several storeys high with elaborate wooden balconies and shutters, stand side by side with new skyscrapers. It is forbidden for non-Muslims to enter the city.

Medina, the second holiest city of Islam, and the place of the Prophet's tomb, lies about 450 kilometres (280 miles) north of Mecca. It also played a central part in early Islamic history.

The Ka'aba—a small square temple in the central courtyard of Mecca's Great Mosque—surrounded by pilgrims in their white robes

The Prophet Muhammad and his followers made their migration there to escape persecution in Mecca in the year A.D. 622. This migration is known in Arabic as the *Hejira* and the year A.D. 622 is considered in the Islamic calendar as year 1. In most of the rest of the world we use what is known as the Gregorian calendar. In the Islamic calendar, the years are shorter by about eleven days. Thus the year 1985 is 1405/1406 in the Islamic calendar. In modern Saudi Arabia, newspapers carry both dates.

Medina has also existed since ancient times and has benefited

The Prophet's Mosque in Medina

from the pilgrim trade. In addition, the city lies in a fertile oasis area and has long cultivated large plantations of dates and other crops. A visit to the Prophet's Mosque is the main purpose of pilgrimage to Medina. As in Mecca, entry into the city is forbidden to non-Muslims.

Jeddah is the largest city in the western region. It is primarily a port city and throughout its long history it has been the gateway to Mecca. As recently as the 1940s, Jeddah was a small, walled town with only a few tens of thousands of inhabitants. The Jeddah of today is a sprawling metropolis with over a million people. In the 1920s there was only one single tree standing within the city walls. Today, trees, grass, flowers and tropical plants abound everywhere as a startling symbol of the growth and vitality of Jeddah. The King Abdul Aziz International

Airport is now the main point of entry for pilgrims. The airport contains the famous Hajj Terminal, designed to cope with the huge flow of people. The Terminal is the largest covered space in the world and its tent-shaped roofs echo the shapes of the traditional pilgrims' tents.

Jeddah used to be known as the City of the Consuls, and was the most open of Arabia's towns. Now it is the most cosmopolitan city in the kingdom and the majority of its inhabitants are foreigners. It is also in Jeddah and the surrounding regions that the wide diversity of the Saudi character can be seen. A Saudi citizen today may have the classic appearance of the desert Arab, or may be of black African stock, or may be oriental with Chinese features. The Saudi Arabian people comprise both pilgrims from far and wide who remained and became naturalized citizens and also the descendants of

The Hajj Terminal, Jeddah Airport

black slaves. Jeddah continues to be a melting-pot of people and cultures.

It is also a city of freeways, modern architecture and tower blocks. Many of the new small factories and manufacturing concerns are located here. In recognition of the city's relationship with the sea, the entire length of Jeddah's shoreline, the Corniche, is being developed as a leisure area. Parks, gardens, beaches, fountains, public sculptures, restaurants, cafés and sports complexes now line the Red Sea shore and make the Corniche the city's most popular entertainment area.

The people of Jeddah are proud of their heritage. The ancient heart of the city, the Old Town, is now being preserved. The buildings reflect the city's location and history; many are made from coral stone taken from the nearby coral reef. There are

A view of the tower blocks of the commercial district of central Jeddah, the most cosmopolitan city in Saudi Arabia

Traditional architecture in Jeddah Old Town

numerous old caravanserai—hostels for the merchants, travellers and pilgrims of yesteryear. The Old Town, with its twisting alleys, spice markets and historic houses with intricate balconies, is now a conservation area. More than that, it is a constant reminder of old Arabia before the discovery of the oil. All around the old heart of Jeddah is the commercial centre of the city with the concrete, steel and glass of the modern world towering above the older world of coral stone and wood.

Taif, about two hours' drive from Jeddah on a spectacular new mountain road, is a hill town and a summer resort. The cool mountain breezes provide a welcome escape from the intense summer heat. The town is near Mecca and lies about 1,800 metres (5,500 feet) above sea level. The population of 70,000 are mostly engaged in market trading, and servicing the hotel and holiday industry. The *souks* contain gold markets, spice markets and carpet markets; many of the items on sale have been brought by pilgrims from other lands. Taif is the summer capital for the King, the royal princes and the government.

To the north of Jeddah is the port of Yanbu. Until recently, Yanbu was a small, Red Sea fishing town with coral stone houses and little local trade. The Saudi Government has decided to develop Yanbu into a major new industrial city. The plan is to build a city of 130,000 people with major industries involving oil refining, gas processing and petrochemicals and plastics. More than 30,000 labourers from over forty countries are now involved in transforming this quiet, old town into an industrial city. Houses, roads, hospitals, schools and light industries have already been completed. A new airport and industrial seaport are also operational. Like Jubail in the east, Yanbu is a living symbol of the new stage of Saudi development.

THE CENTRAL REGION—THE NAJD

When Ibn Saud and his warriors captured Riyadh in 1902 it

A general view of Riyadh, the Saudi Arabian capital

was not much more than a small town or village, built of mud and isolated deep in the heart of central Arabia. Even by the late 1940s, after the establishment of Saudi Arabia as a nation and Riyadh as a capital, its population was not much over 50,000. Today, it is a city of over one million. Riyadh is the political and administrative capital of the kingdom. It is a city of motorways and flyovers, universities, Government ministries, and television and communication centres. All the foreign embassies and consulates are in the process of moving from Jeddah into a giant diplomatic quarter in Riyadh. The airport is the largest in the world. Highways stretch from Riyadh across the desert to the other parts of Saudi Arabia. The isolation of

1902 is now a distant memory. Indeed, the only physical reminder of the old Riyadh is the mud-walled fort which Ibn Saud captured. It is now carefully preserved in the heart of the city, but it is overshadowed by the new, modern, dynamic Riyadh. Many of the public buildings and royal palaces echo Arab traditions in design and architecture. The massive King Saud University is located in Riyadh. It is one of the largest universities in the whole Arab world with nearly 20,000 students from about seventy countries. There are nearly 5,000 women students, reflecting the growing part women are beginning to play in Saudi society. With its places of learning, its ministries and its communications centres, Riyadh is now a capital of world importance.

THE EASTERN REGION—HASA

About 500 kilometres (300 miles) to the east of Riyadh is the group of cities and towns which make up the centre of the oil industry—Dammam, Dhahran and Al-Khobar. Dammam is the largest seaport on the Arabian Gulf and it is in this coastal area that many of the oil-storage tanks, refineries, tanker terminals and pipelines can be found. The main oil town is Dhahran. Curiously, the strongest influence here is American. Aramco, the Arabian American Oil Company, has its headquarters here and Dhahran is almost a company town, even in its appearance. Some people have described it as being like an American town in Arizona or Texas. Some of the developments here have been due to Aramco's planning on behalf of its giant workforce. Many of the first schools and training colleges were founded here. Just outside Dhahran is the University of Petroleum and Minerals, the kingdom's main teaching and research centre for science and technology. While most of the students are Saudi, the language of instruction is English.

The new industrial city of Jubail is 100 kilometres (60 miles) north of Dhahran. It is still in the process of being built. By the end of the century it will be home to over 350,000 people and the centre of Saudi Arabia's plan to create new areas of manufacturing, thus satisfying many of the kingdom's needs and helping further to reduce dependence on foreign imports.

The distinctive architecture of the town of Najran

Elsewhere in Saudi Arabia, other important towns include Tabuk, the most northerly city near the border with Jordan. In the south-west, near Yemen, are the attractive towns of Abha and Najran. Their architecture is extremely beautiful. Many of the buildings are enormous, tall mud-brick structures, with castellated towers and white-painted geometric designs. Because of the scenery and architecture, the south-west region, the Asir, is being developed as a major tourist attraction with national parks, museums, craft centres and wildlife parks.

The towns and cities of Saudi Arabia encompass the ancient and the new, the industrial and the religious. The one unifying factor is that all have changed dramatically in the last forty years. In their individual ways, the cities reflect the story of modern Saudi Arabia.

Saudi Arabia: The Present and the Future

Saudi Arabia is now the richest and largest country in the Arab world. Indeed, its economic power is so great that its influence is now felt throughout the whole world—in the advanced countries of the West and in the developing countries of the Third World. In some ways, the experience of Saudi Arabia in the last fifty years seems like a giant experiment: a meeting between the modern, technological world of the twentieth century and a way of life unchanged for hundreds, if not thousands, of years. It is perhaps impossible to judge the success of this experiment. The invasion of the outside world and of modernity into this deeply traditional and conservative society has produced many stresses and strains. The fierce sense of family and tribal identity, coupled with the deep-rooted belief in Islam, have given a strong foundation to Saudi life. These factors have helped Saudi Arabia withstand the most severe shocks of sudden modernity.

The major problem has been the need constantly to face new dilemmas: the pace of the modern world is such that there is no breathing-space. In Europe, the general development of the societies we live in has happened over the space of centuries. To Saudi Arabians, this must seem almost leisurely.

Considering Saudi Arabia's past, the nature of its inhabitants and its society, and the explosive growth of the last few decades, the progress and achievements so far must be admired. And yet, after oil, there is one resource which Saudi Arabia must use if it is to guarantee a prosperous future for itself, namely its own population. At present there is an official policy in effect which is known as Saudi-ization. It could be said that this is the real revolution within Saudi society. Until now, the majority of jobs were done by foreign workers. Now, strict limits are being applied on the number of foreign workers permitted to work in the kingdom. The aim of the policy of Saudi-ization is the gradual taking over of most of the important jobs by Saudi Arabians.

Extensive in-service training schemes have been instituted in offices, workplaces and organizations to groom Saudis in the necessary skills. The Government is investing heavily in education. Universities are expanding and training and vocational centres are springing up all over the country. There will continue to be a large foreign workforce, composed mainly of Asians and Yemenis, to do most of the manual work. The challenge for the Saudi Government and the Saudi people is whether they can take over the running of their country and work as hard and effectively as those who have done it until now. The Saudis are recognizing the fact that, being privileged

Students in Riyadh's College of Agriculture, part of the Government's expansion of vocational training to speed Saudi-ization

recipients of the oil wealth, they also have major responsibilities.

In a wider context, Saudi Arabia has also recognized the need for regional co-operation to ensure political stability. The Middle East is a very troubled part of the world and the continued security of the oil-producing nations is a concern for the world at large. In 1981, the Gulf Co-operation Council (the GCC) was formed. This is an alliance between Saudi Arabia and the neighbouring countries of Bahrain, Qatar, the United Arab Emirates, Oman and Kuwait. Its aims are to foster security, encourage trade co-operation and develop closer links in other fields. The Iran–Iraq war has brought into sharp focus the dangers which threaten the area and the oil supplies.

Internationally, Saudi Arabia exercises great responsibility as a major member of the Organization of Petroleum Exporting Countries (OPEC). The industrial West relies heavily upon oil to maintain its economies and Saudi Arabia is crucial in regulating both the price and the supply. As a consequence of its massive economic influence, Saudi Arabia has been able to assume a stronger role in international politics. In particular, the kingdom is most concerned about a settlement to the Arab-Israeli conflict and the Palestinian problem. Saudi Arabia's main desire is that Israel should withdraw from occupied Arab territories, including the holy city of Jerusalem, as a prelude to a peaceful settlement of the issues.

Saudi Arabia still faces many challenges. The Government is determined to create an economy based on new industries as well as oil. This will both reduce the dependence on oil revenues and decrease foreign imports of other commodities. At the same time, Saudi Arabians are being trained to take over the running and working of their country. Within the region, and internationally, the prime concern is for continued stability and a settlement of Middle East conflicts such as the Iran-Iraq war, the war in Lebanon and the Arab-Israeli conflict.

The main aim of Saudi Arabians is that their country should continue to progress carefully, accepting what is good and necessary from the outside world, but preserving the essential Saudi and Islamic character of their own world.

Index

Abdul Aziz Ibn Saud *see* Ibn Saud
Abha 88
agriculture 16, 21, 74-75
airports 58, 80-81, 84
Al-Khobar 86
Al-Rashid tribe 37-38
Al-Saud tribe 31, 37, 41
Arabia Deserta 11
Arabian Gulf 20, 32-33, 40, 42, 69, 72-73, 86
Arabian Peninsula 7, 11, 31
Arabic language 23-24, 40, 57-58
Aramco 68-69, 86-87
Asir 15-16, 18, 88

Babylon 34
Bahrain 69, 91
Bedouin 8, 18, 20, 38, 48-55
Britain, British Government 7, 40, 42

Cairo 8, 43
camels 8, 15, 54-55
caravans, caravanserai 8, 83
Christians, Christianity 24, 26-27
city life 56-57, 77-88
coffee 53, 60
conservation 83
construction 21, 73-74

Damascus 35
Dammam 21, 57, 86
dates, date palms 16-17, 20, 59
Dhahran 21, 42, 68, 86-87
desalination 71-72
driving 64-65

education 86, 90
Egypt, Egyptians 8, 14, 25, 33-34, 43-44
Eid al Fitr 26

Empty Quarter 18
Ethiopia 14
Europe, Europeans 8, 12, 25, 57, 69
explorers 18, 36

Fahd, King 46
family life 52-53
Farouk, King of Egypt 44
Feisal, King 44, 45, 46
First World War 39
food 53-54, 59-61

gold 21
Gulf Co-operation Council (GCC) 91

Hajj 25, 30, 78
Hajj Terminal 81
Hasa 20, 86-88
Hejaz 13-15, 18, 39, 77-84
Hussein 39

Ibn Saud, King 8, 31-32, 36-43, 85
Ikhwan 38-39
imports 45
India 7, 11, 25, 32, 35
Iran 42, 91-92
Iraq 18, 42, 91-92
Islam 8, 22-30, 35, 37, 40, 47, 89, 92
Israel 45-46, 92

Jeddah 13, 15, 40, 56-58, 69, 72-73, 79-84
Jerusalem 45, 92
Jews, Judaism 24, 26-27
Jordan 13, 88
Jubail 72, 84, 87

Ka'aba 78
Khalid, King 46

93

King Saud University 86
Kings of Saudi Arabia,
— Abdul Aziz Ibn Saud *see* Ibn Saud
— Saud 43
— Feisal 44, 45, 46
— Khalid 46
— Fahd 46

Korea, Koreans 58, 74
Kuwait 37, 91

Lawrence of Arabia 39
Lebanon 42, 92

Madain Saleh 33, 35
majlis 51
marriage 40-41, 52, 65-66
Mecca 7, 13-15, 22-25, 34-35, 40, 57, 77-78
Medina 7, 15, 22-24, 32, 34, 40, 57, 78-80
Mediterranean 33, 69
minerals 21, 73
mosques 22, 24, 29, 78, 80
Muhammad 22-30, 35
Muslims 23-30, 36, 57-58, 67, 77-78, 80

Nabataeans 33
Nafud Desert 18, 20
Najd 20, 37, 39, 84-85
Najran 88
Nasser, Gamal Abdul 43
national flag 22
natural gas 72-73
new industries 73, 84
nomads *see* Bedouin

oases 8, 15, 77
oil 8, 21, 42, 68-73, 91-92
OPEC (Organization of Petroleum Exporting Countries) 92
Ottoman Empire 8, 35, 37, 39

Palestine, Palestinians 34, 45-46, 92
petrochemicals 84
pilgrims 7, 15, 25, 78
pipelines 42, 68
plants 16, 20, 80
political system 46-47
population 11, 15

Quran 23-30, 38, 46-47

raids 49, 53
rainfall 13, 16
Ramadan 25-26
Ras Tanura 69
Red Sea 7, 8, 11, 13-14, 21, 32, 40, 69, 72
Riyadh 20, 31, 37, 40, 56, 76, 84-85
Romans 11, 33
Rub-al-Khali *see* Empty Quarter

Salat 24
Saud, King 43
Saudia airlines 43
Saudi dress 61-62
Saudi-ization 90
Shahada 23, 24
Sharia Law 27
sheikhs 51
Shia Muslims 29
souks 63-64, 84
Spain 8, 35
spice route 14-15, 33
sports 64
Sudan 15
Suez Canal 7
Sunni Muslims 29
Syria 35

Tabuk 15, 88
Taif 15, 43, 84
telecommunications 75-76
Turks 8, 35, 37-38